D0607553

in the news™

SAFETY AND THE FOOD SUPPLY

Laura La Bella

ROSEN
PUBLISHING®

New York

Published in 2009 by The Rosen Publishing Group, Inc.
29 East 21st Street, New York, NY 10010

Library of Congress Cataloging-in-Publication Data

La Bella, Laura.
Safety and the food supply / Laura La Bella.
     p. cm.—(In the news)
Includes bibliographical references and index.
ISBN-13: 978-1-4358-5036-1 (library binding)
ISBN-13: 978-1-4358-5364-5 (pbk)
ISBN-13: 978-1-4358-5370-6 (6 pack)
1. Food—United States—Safety measures—Juvenile literature. 2. Food supply—Health aspects—United States—Juvenile literature. 3. Food industry and trade—Safety regulations—United States—Juvenile literature. I. Title.
RA601.L3 2009
363.19'20973—dc22

                                                            2008013410

Manufactured in Malaysia

On the cover: Clockwise from top left: Fresh fruit for sale at a farmer's market; a technician tests for *E. coli* contamination; greenhouse plants are sprayed with insecticides.

contents

Protecting Food from Farm to Fork

W here does food come from? If you guess the supermarket, you're half right. But where does the food that lines the shelves of supermarkets come from? It's grown and raised on farms all across America and the world beyond. Shiny red apples, ripe yellow bananas, and lush green beans; grain used to make flour for breads, crackers, and cereals; and cattle and chicken raised for their milk and meat all come from farms and plantations.

The United States is the largest producer of food in the world. Agriculture is one of America's largest industries, with more than twenty million people working in agriculture-related jobs. These jobs range from farm workers who grow crops and raise animals to agricultural inspectors, equipment operators, and graders and sorters who examine foods that are going to be sold to the public. The United States produces so much food that it exports, or sends to other countries, more than $60 billion worth of agricultural products each year. These products

Within a supermarket, you can find all types of foods from around the world, including fruits, vegetables, dairy products, and grains like cereals and breads. Before all this food appears on the shelf, it must pass food safety guidelines to make sure it is safe to eat.

include everything from fruits and vegetables to meats, grains, crackers, pasta, soda, and milk.

Keeping this vast supply of food safe is very important. Food safety is more about making sure that foods stay fresh while traveling from farms to super-markets and, ultimately, to your kitchen table. It's about making sure foods are labeled so consumers, or those buying foods, know what ingredients are in products. It's ensuring that foods are manufactured in clean environments, that foods don't contain additives that could cause illness, and that even the packaging the food comes in is safe.

There are two federal organizations that make sure the foods we eat are safe. They are the Food and Drug Administration (FDA) and the Food Safety and Inspection Service (FSIS). These two organizations set all the rules and regulations for food and food safety in the United States. The FDA oversees all foods produced in the United States, except for meat and poultry, which is monitored by FSIS, an office within the U.S. Department of Agriculture (USDA). Thanks to these two organizations, the U.S. food supply is one of the safest in the world.

Protecting Your Health

The FDA is a large government agency that protects the health of the public. In addition to enforcing food safety regulations, it also monitors the production of drugs, biological products, medical devices, and makeup and skin care products. The FDA is responsible for creating new ways to make medicine safer and more affordable. It also makes sure the public is informed of ways they can use medicine and food to improve their health.

The FDA's Center for Food Safety and Applied Nutrition (CFSAN) is the main arm of the agency that oversees the American food supply. CFSAN protects the

The FDA has a number of advisory committees that meet with leaders in different industries and make recommendations on products.

public by making sure foods are safe to eat, are produced in clean environments, are nutritionally wholesome, and are labeled honestly. The center does this by enforcing the regulations imposed on the companies that produce foods in the United States, as well as on food companies that want to sell their products in America. CFSAN has a number of important objectives to ensure food safety, such as:

- Inspecting food production establishments and food warehouses. Samples of foods produced in these facilities are collected and analyzed for different types of contamination.

- Reviewing the safety of food and color additives.
- Reviewing the drugs used to keep animals—like chickens, pigs, and cows—healthy in order to ensure the safety of the animals that receive them and the humans who will eventually eat food produced by these animals.
- Monitoring the safety of the food that animals eat.
- Developing rules, guidelines, and regulations for restaurants and grocery stores that prepare foods.
- Establishing safe and healthy food manufacturing practices and other production standards, like plant sanitation and packaging requirements.
- Working with foreign governments to ensure the safety of food products that are imported, or brought in from other countries.
- Requesting that manufacturers recall unsafe food products and monitoring those recalls when foods are found to cause illness.
- Conducting research on food safety to ensure that the best practices are in place and widely used.
- Educating both the industry and consumers on safe food handling practices.

The FSIS is another public health agency. This organization, which is an office within the USDA, is responsible for guaranteeing that meat, poultry, eggs, and egg products are safe, wholesome, and correctly labeled and packaged.

An Exposé Leads to Reform

How did the FDA and FSIS come about? It was actually a book that raised awareness of the food industry and the terrible working conditions for many of its employees. In 1905, Upton Sinclair, a well-known author, published a novel called *The Jungle.* The book examined the horrible, unsanitary, and dangerous conditions in a Chicago meatpacking house and throughout the meatpacking industry, and it raised public concern for the safety of the meat produced by them.

Sinclair's novel got the attention of U.S. president Theodore Roosevelt, who asked that inspectors begin to work in the meatpacking houses. After seeing firsthand the terrible conditions, the inspectors suggested that new rules be placed on meatpacking companies to clean their warehouses and maintain a new level of health for their workers. They also established laws on how to best handle meat in safe ways. The laws, called the Pure Food and Drug Act and the Meat Inspection Act, were passed in 1906. These laws have since been revised, but they still govern many aspects of the food industry today.

Upton Sinclair's book *The Jungle* took a look inside the working conditions of a meatpacking house in Chicago. The book caught the attention of President Theodore Roosevelt, who enacted laws that protected the workers and helped establish guidelines for safer food practices.

The FDA and the FSIS focus many of their efforts on three key areas: prevention, partnerships, and inspection resources. Prevention is key if food is to be grown, shipped, and sold in safe ways. Many of the rules in place help to reduce the chance of illness before a risk can even be created. Both organizations work to build effective partnerships with farmers, meatpacking houses, and even other countries that may send their food to the United States. And, finally, if rules are going to be in place, someone needs to enforce them. That's what food inspectors do. The FDA and the FISI make sure inspectors have the resources they need to do their jobs effectively.

National Food Safety Programs

The FDA has put into place a number of food safety programs to educate the public on the best ways to

2111536300223A
BEST BY JUN292007

Food labeling laws require companies to post dates on their products to indicate when it's safe to eat a particular food.

keep foods safe and how best to keep bacteria from forming on foods, and to raise awareness of food safety issues (like nutrition labels). Here are just a few of the FDA's food safety programs:

- Spot the Block was created to educate children on how to use the nutrition labels to better manage their diets. The program's goal is to help prevent obesity in tweens (kids between the ages of eight and thirteen), help prevent health problems in adulthood, and encourage healthier eating. Spot the Block teaches kids how to read a food label; understand what a healthy serving size of a food is; choose healthy, nutritional foods; and consider the calories of each food.
- Fight BAC! is a campaign that teaches how best to keep bacteria from developing on food. According to both the FDA and FSIS, bacteria

This Fight BAC! poster shows consumers how to clean, separate, chill, and cook foods to ensure they remain safe for consumption. Fight BAC! is a national campaign that teaches how best to keep bacteria from developing on food.

that cause foodborne illness grow most rapidly in warmer temperatures. That's why it is important to keep your refrigerator at 40° Fahrenheit (4.4° Celsius) or below. This is one of the most effective ways to reduce the risk of bacteria growth and the resulting illnesses that can follow. The Fight BAC! campaign raises awareness of the importance of proper food handling at home.

- Food Safety Education Month is held each year during the month of September, when students are returning for the new school year. Each year, restaurants and the food service industry raise awareness of the importance of food safety education. Games that teach the importance of washing your hands, cleaning fruits and veg-etables before eating them, and safe cooking methods are promoted to schools nationwide.

Is What You Are Eating Safe?

A very important role the FDA plays in maintaining food safety concerns the labels you see on packaged food. Food labeling and nutritional information keep you aware of what's in the food you buy. They also tell you how healthy that food is. Food labeling is required for most prepared foods, like breads, cereals, canned and frozen foods, snacks, desserts, and drinks. Food labels contain information such as serving size, calories, and fat content, as well as nutrient information.

There are also important dates on food packaging that tell you when it's safe to eat a particular food. These are called "Best before" or "Use by" dates. "Best before" dates are used on items of food to show you when a food should be eaten by. For example, go to your pantry or cupboard and look at a package of crackers or cookies. There will be a date on it that says "Best before . . ." These dates indicate the date by which an item has outlived its shelf life. Many foods, drinks, and other perishable items are given a "Best before" date, which means the food is best if eaten by these dates. You might be able to eat those cookies in your pantry even if it is after the "Best before" date, but they may not be as fresh.

Another term you might see is "Use by." This term is a little bit different than the term "Best before." "Use by" means that a product is no longer safe to eat after the specified date listed on the package. These products, like milk or meat, are more likely to cause illness if they are eaten after the "Use by" date. After this date, the product has most likely gone bad and is not healthy for you to eat or drink.

The Government's Role in Food Safety

2

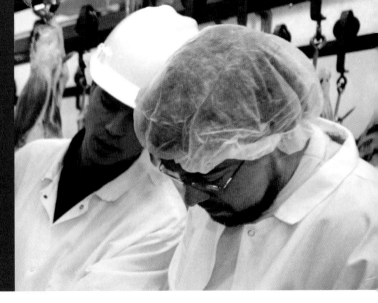

More than a century ago, the kitchen looked much different than it does today. Take a look at your refrigerator. It's a marvel of engineering: a large box with shelves and compartments that keep foods consistently cool. A century ago, kitchens looked much different. Even how people ate was much different.

The beginning of the twentieth century is a time that marks the beginning of significant change in the food industry. In the early 1900s, there were no refrigerators, at least not how we know them today. Instead, you owned an icebox. On a regular basis, a deliveryman brought to your home a large chunk of ice, which you placed in a large wooden box. The walls of the icebox were lined with sawdust, cork, or straw. This helped to keep the cold from the ice inside the icebox.

The icebox was an invention that came from the growth of industry. In the 1900s, the Unites States was changing as a nation. During the Industrial Revolution,

In 1936, when ice boxes kept food cold, workers would deliver large bricks of ice to homes on a regular basis.

industries such as textiles and steel were growing rapidly, and cities began to spring up all around the country. Soon, it became necessary for food to be brought into these cities from farms located in more rural areas. This presented farmers with a problem. How could they keep foods, like meat, milk, and eggs, cold while in transit to cities? And how could these items stay cold in people's homes? This was how the icebox was invented.

The History of Government Intervention in Food Safety

During this same time period, as industries and cities grew, conditions in the U.S. food and drug industries were unregulated. Because there was not the scientific knowledge about food and drug dangers then that we have now, there was widespread use of chemical preservatives and toxic colors used on meats and produce.

This was when Upton Sinclair's novel *The Jungle* brought about change in the meat industry. Sinclair revealed to a shocked and disgusted public the conditions in meatpacking plants. He also highlighted widespread use of poisonous preservatives and dyes in foods and exposed the false claims drug makers made for worthless and dangerous medicines. All of these revelations resulted in the creation of two Congressional acts designed to bring about change in the food industry. The Meat Inspection Act and the Pure Food and Drug Act were passed in 1906. Both of these acts outlined new federal laws that allowed for the inspection of meat products and forbade the manufacture, sale, or transportation of altered food products or poisonous medicines. The laws also prohibited individuals or companies from adding ingredients that were food substitutes, that concealed damage to a food, or that posed a health hazard to consumers.

A field inspector from the Department of Agriculture in Washington State inspects the operations at Island Grown Farmers Cooperative to make sure the plant meets state regulations for meat processing facilities.

Shortly after these laws went into effect, the FDA as we know it was established.

The FDA and FSIS

The FDA has grown into a large governmental body that regulates the labeling and safety of food items. It also oversees the drug industry (product approvals, over-the-counter and prescription drug labeling, and drug manufacturing standards), veterinary products (pet foods and drugs used for animal health), makeup and cosmetics, medical devices (approval of new devices, manufacturing and performance standards, and tracking reports of malfunctioning devices), and any products that give off radiation (all types of X-ray machines, tanning beds, and microwaves).

In addition to the Meat Inspection Act and the Pure Food and Drug Act, there were several additional amendments and laws that were passed to reshape how the food industry worked. Two especially important early laws were enacted. The Sherley Amendment made it illegal to label medicines with false claims intended to defraud consumers. The Gould Amendment required food packaging that clearly listed the contents of the food item, including its weight, measure, or numerical count.

As noted in chapter 1, the FSIS is a public health agency within the U.S. Department of Agriculture (USDA). The USDA develops and executes policy on farming, agriculture, and food. It works to accomplish a number of missions, including meeting the needs of farmers and ranchers, promoting agricultural trade and production, working to assure food safety, protecting natural resources, and fostering rural communities. The FSIS is the arm of the USDA that is responsible for ensuring that the nation's commercial supply of meat, poultry, and egg products is safe, wholesome, and correctly labeled and packaged.

The FSIS has two advisory committees. The National Advisory Committee on Meat and Poultry Inspection advises the U.S. secretary of agriculture on matters affecting federal and state inspection program activities. The National Advisory Committee on Microbiological Criteria for Foods provides scientific advice to federal food safety agencies. These agencies use the information from this advisory committee to develop an integrated national food safety system that guarantees the safety of food from farms all the way to consumers who purchase these foods. They also ensure the safety of domestic, imported, and exported foods.

Other Food Agencies at Work

In addition to the FDA and the FSIS, there are a number of other agencies that support the efforts of food safety. For example, the Centers for Disease Control and Prevention (CDC) is the nation's premiere health promotion, prevention, and preparedness agency and a global leader in public health. The CDC remains at the forefront of public health efforts to prevent and control infectious and chronic diseases, injuries, workplace hazards, disabilities, and environmental health threats.

Preventing foodborne illness and death remains a major public health challenge for the agency. As a result, the CDC has a number of food safety activities and programs in place to raise public awareness of preventable foodborne illness. These activities and programs include publications, partnerships with other government agencies and companies within the food industry, extensive Web sites to spread information, networks of health officials and health organizations, and monitoring systems to track illness outbreaks nationwide.

The Organic Consumers Association is an organization that campaigns for health, justice, and sustainability for organic consumers. It's the only organization in the United States that focuses only on promoting the views of the more than fifty million organic consumers. The organization represents more than 850,000 members, including thousands of businesses that manufacture or sell organic foods. Over the last eight years, the Organic Consumers Association has worked with its members to pressure both the USDA and organic food companies to preserve strict organic standards for growing and selling foods.

The International Association for Food Protection has a membership of more than three thousand people who work in the areas of food protection, industry, and the government. Its members keep informed of the latest scientific, technical, and practical developments in food safety and sanitation. The association also produces two scientific journals, *Food Protection Trends* and the *Journal of Food Protection*, both of which feature the latest information and research on the rapidly changing technologies, innovations, and regulations in food safety.

The Food Safety Information Center specializes in providing food safety information to educators, industry, researchers, and the general public. The center was established at the USDA's National Agricultural Library in 2003 as a way to efficiently use library resources, develop stronger collaborations among the library's food safety programs, and, ultimately, deliver the best possible services to the food safety community.

The Center for Science in the Public Interest is an organization that ensures that government regulators, policymakers, and members of the food industry work harder to protect American consumers from food contamination. The organization works to strengthen current food safety laws and adopt new ones to protect American consumers.

National Food Safety Education Month

To raise awareness of food safety in school-aged children, the National Restaurant Association Educational Foundation's International Food Safety Council created National Food Safety Education Month. According to the organization's Web site, the purpose of this event is to "focus public attention on foodborne illness and the safe food handling practices consumers can follow to

National Food Safety Education Month helps to raise awareness of food safety in school-aged children. The month-long campaign was created by the National Restaurant Association Educational Foundation's International Food Safety Council.

stay healthy." This annual campaign for restaurants and the food service industry stresses the importance of food safety education. Each year, a new theme is selected and training activities are created to reinforce proper food safety practices and procedures. Training activities include food safety fairs, contests, parades, exhibits, workshops, educational fairs, and supermarket tours.

Food Scares

With all the rules and regulations in place, there are still times when a food safety hazard occurs. Between the efforts of companies that make food products and the government's enforcing of proper food safety techniques, our food supply is extremely safe. But accidents and mistakes do happen.

The Peanut Butter Scare

On February 14, 2007, the FDA announced that a nationwide *Salmonella* outbreak had occurred. *Salmonella* is a form of bacteria that causes salmonellosis, one of the most common intestinal infections in the United States. People who had eaten Peter Pan and Great Value brand peanut butter started to get sick. They reported symptoms such as stomach cramps, fever, nausea, and vomiting. The FDA asked ConAgra, the company that makes these brands of peanut butter, to recall the products. A product recall is when a company asks stores that carry its item

These jars of Peter Pan peanut butter were recalled due to an outbreak of *Salmonella*. Around the country, grocery stores pulled the peanut butter jars from their shelves and consumers threw out thousands of jars of the contaminated peanut butter.

to take it off their shelves so that it can no longer be purchased. The FDA also alerted the media, which helped to spread awareness of the outbreak to people around the country.

Scientists tested both brands of peanut butter and confirmed that the products were contaminated with *Salmonella*. ConAgra conducted its own investigation into the outbreak and found that moisture might have triggered the growth of the bacteria. It was determined that moisture in the company's production facility could have allowed the growth of *Salmonella* organisms that were likely already present in raw peanuts or peanut dust. The investigation also found that the moisture could have come from a roof that leaked during a rainstorm and from a faulty sprinkler system that went off twice. As many as 628 people in forty-seven states were affected by the *Salmonella* in these two peanut butter products.

Poisonous Produce

In the fall of 2006, three hospitals in California began to see patients with symptoms that suggested they had been infected with *Escherichia coli*, or *E. coli*. This is a bacteria commonly found in the lower intestine of humans and other warm-blooded animals. There are many different strains, or types, of *E. coli*. Most are harmless, but a few can become dangerous and even life threatening. This was the case in California when a number of people became sick. As hospitals reported the illnesses, the state's health departments began to investigate. They determined that the source of the *E. coli* outbreak was packaged lettuce and spinach that were pre-mixed and pre-washed. The lettuce and spinach had been shipped to grocery stores around the country. Soon, reports of people sick from *E. coli* were coming from all around the nation. Grocery stores quickly pulled the produce from their shelves and notified consumers of the outbreak.

Mad Cow Disease

Mad cow disease was first discovered in 1986 in cattle raised in Great Britain. It is an incurable, fatal brain disease that affects the nervous system of a cow. The disease causes the animal to act strangely and lose control of its ability to do everyday things such as walk. The disease is spread when cows eat meal that contains the meat and bone of other infected cows. It is believed, but not yet proven, that the disease can be spread to humans, resulting in a degenerative neurological disease known as Creutzfeldt-Jakob disease. The USDA reports there is no evidence that the disease is transmitted through cow's milk and milk products. To date, only three cases of mad cow disease have been reported in the United States, while almost 200,000 cows in England have been sickened and millions were slaughtered as a precaution. As many as 165 people in England developed Creutzfeldt-Jacob disease and died.

A Major Beef Recall

In January 2008, the Humane Society released an undercover video that shows sick cows being treated violently at Hallmark Meat Packing in Chino, California. The cows, many of which were sick or injured, were being slaughtered against regulations by the USDA. The company requested a recall of more than 143 million pounds of beef—the largest beef recall in U.S. history— much of which was supplied to public schools nationwide over a two-year period. Two employees captured on the video now face criminal charges for animal cruelty.

Steven Mendell, CEO of Westland/Hallmark Meat Company, appears in front of the House of Representatives in Washington, D.C., to testify about the release of a videotape showing the violent treatment of sick cows at one of his slaughterhouses. As a result of the video, Westland/Hallmark recalled 143 million pounds of ground beef—the largest ground beef recall in U.S. history.

A Pet Food Recall

Menu Foods, a Canadian pet food manufacturer, recalled a number of varieties of pet food due to reports of cats and dogs getting sick. Testing of the food found that the ingredient wheat gluten was contaminated with a chemical called melamine, which can be poisonous in high doses.

Menu Foods, a Canadian food company, was forced to recall sixty million cans and packages of pet food after many animals became sick from eating the products. The pet food was found to be contaminated with a toxic chemical.

Menu Foods said the wheat gluten was traced to the Xuzhou Anying Biologic Technology Development Company in China. The FDA has blocked additional gluten imports from the company until further investigation, including testing, can be completed. Menu Foods wasn't the only pet food manufacturer affected. Hill's Pet Nutrition, P&G Pet Care, Nestlé Purina PetCare, Del Monte Pet Products, and Sunshine Mills also conducted recalls.

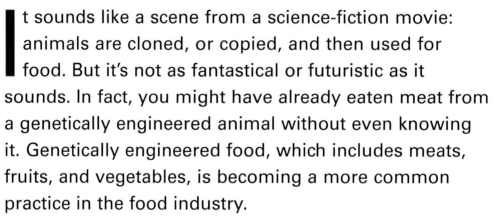

The Controversial Collision of Science and Food

It sounds like a scene from a science-fiction movie: animals are cloned, or copied, and then used for food. But it's not as fantastical or futuristic as it sounds. In fact, you might have already eaten meat from a genetically engineered animal without even knowing it. Genetically engineered food, which includes meats, fruits, and vegetables, is becoming a more common practice in the food industry.

What exactly is genetically engineered food? The explanation involves a short science lesson. Every living organism is made up of DNA, which is like a set of blueprints. Our DNA tells us the color of our eyes, how tall we will grow, if our hair will be straight or curly, and much, much more. When genetically engineering foods, scientists look for the best qualities in produce and animals. They then combine them to create a more perfect food. For example, say a farmer wants to grow corn that needs less water to grow. The farmer will work with scientists to find another plant that does well with

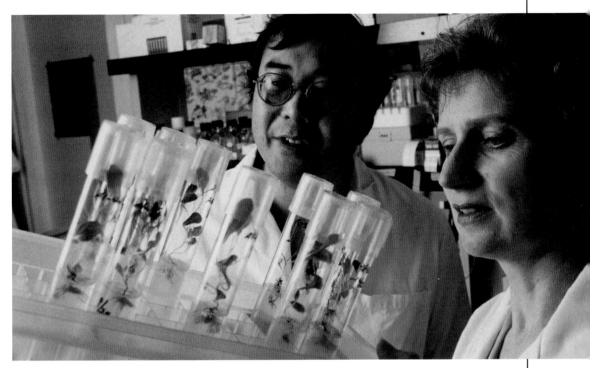

Scientists are creating genetically engineered plants to help aid in the growth of the food supply. The practice, while fascinating, has become controversial.

less water. Once one is found, they extract the appropriate dry-weather gene from the hardy plant, insert it into corn seed, and plant the seed. Several months later, the farmer now has corn that is genetically engineered to grow even if enough water is not always available.

These genetically engineered foods were first made available to consumers in the early 1990s. Currently, the most common genetically engineered foods are soybeans, corn, canola and cottonseed oils, and wheat. Almost 45 percent of corn and 85 percent of soybeans grown in the United States are genetically engineered. It has been estimated that up to 75 percent of processed foods on supermarket shelves—from soda to soup, crackers to condiments—contain genetically engineered ingredients.

There is much controversy over genetically engineered foods. Many say there are benefits, including resistance to pests and disease and an increase in tolerance to drought, herbicide, and cold. However, there are many arguments against these foods, too. Some say they present environmental hazards, can be harmful to the animals that may feed on them, and pose a high risk for an increase in allergies in humans.

Genetically Cloned Animals

If genetically engineered food isn't strange enough to think about, some farms are now cloning animals. Just like produce that can be engineered, animals can be cloned. An animal clone is an exact copy of the original animal, similar to an identical twin, but born at a different time. Cloning is different from genetic engineering, which involves altering, adding, or deleting DNA.

While cloning is very controversial, the FDA announced in January 2008 that, after extensive testing and analysis, meat and milk from cloned cattle, pigs, goats, and the offspring of these clones are as safe to eat as food from conventionally bred animals. The purpose of cloning animals is to improve the value of a herd of cattle or pigs, resulting in animals that produce higher-quality milk and meat. Critics worry that humans may become susceptible to new and unforeseen infections and diseases that may arise due to cloning. Foods from these animals are not expected to be on supermarket shelves for at least several years.

Ben and Jerry's, the famous ice cream company, organized a march through the streets of Washington, D.C., in opposition to the genetic engineering of cows. The company is famous for using hormone-free milk in all of its products.

Food Irradiation

Food irradiation is a process in which foods are exposed to radiant energy, including gamma rays, electron beams, and X-rays, which reduces harmful bacteria in the food. Irradiation is an important food safety tool in fighting foodborne illness. While it may sound cutting-edge, this technique is not new. In 1963, the FDA found irradiated food to be safe. While irradiation is not a substitute for good sanitation and process control in meat and poultry

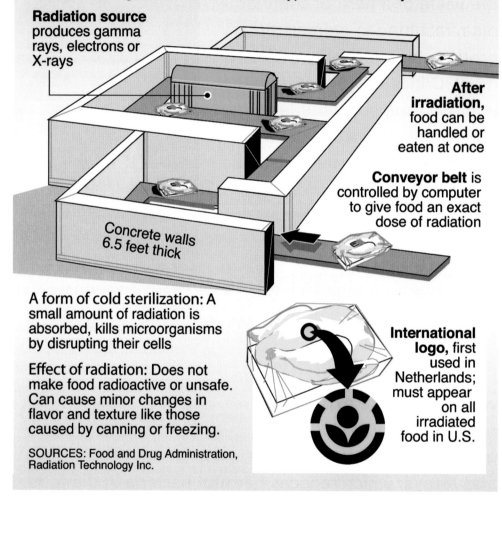

Killing germs in meat with radiation

The Agriculture Department has approved the use of radiation to kill disease-causing bacteria in red meat. A typical irradiation system:

Radiation source produces gamma rays, electrons or X-rays

After irradiation, food can be handled or eaten at once

Conveyor belt is controlled by computer to give food an exact dose of radiation

Concrete walls 6.5 feet thick

A form of cold sterilization: A small amount of radiation is absorbed, kills microorganisms by disrupting their cells

Effect of radiation: Does not make food radioactive or unsafe. Can cause minor changes in flavor and texture like those caused by canning or freezing.

International logo, first used in Netherlands; must appear on all irradiated food in U.S.

SOURCES: Food and Drug Administration, Radiation Technology Inc.

This diagram of a typical food irradiation system explains how the process works.

plants, it is argued that it can add another layer of safety to our food. Many people worry about the long-term health consequences of ingesting food that has been irradiated. The government insists the process is safe.

Milk has been pasteurized for years. Pasteurization destroys harmful bacteria, making milk safer to drink. Irradiation works in the same way, making meat and poultry safer by reducing the number of harmful bacteria and parasites. Irradiation of meat and poultry is done in a government-approved irradiation facility. The amounts of radiant energy that are applied to foods are not strong enough to cause foods to become radioactive. Scientific studies show that irradiation does not significantly change the nutrient content, flavor, or texture of food.

Currently, fresh meat and poultry (including skinless poultry, pork chops, roasts, stew meat, liver, hamburgers, ground meat, and ground poultry) are approved for irradiation. U.S. food regulations also allow the irradiation of wheat and wheat powder, white potatoes, many spices, dry vegetable seasonings, fresh shell eggs, and fresh produce.

Pesticides

A pesticide is a substance used to prevent, control, or lessen the damage caused by a pest. Most pests, such as insects, eat fruits and vegetables. Pesticides are used to keep these bugs away and keep produce healthy. The Environmental Protection Agency (EPA) has a pesticides program that does a number of things, like evaluating new pesticides and their uses, reviewing the safety of older pesticides, registering companies that produce or sell these products, and enforcing the use of pesticides. Because pesticides are designed to kill insects and are often toxic, many consumers worry about eating food treated with pesticides. Links between some kinds of pesticides and various cancers have been established. As a result, the organic food movement is growing strong.

You may have heard about organic food. Any foods that are grown, like fruits, vegetables, and grains used for baking, are considered organic if they were grown without the use of pesticides or artificial fertilizers. It also means no food additives were used. For animals, it means they were raised without the use of antibiotics or growth hormones. Organic foods are growing in popularity and can now be found on almost all supermarket shelves.

Preventing Foodborne Illness

Even though farmers and food companies follow strict rules on how food should be handled, you should be knowledgeable about how to keep yourself from getting sick. After all, we are all in charge of making sure that whatever we eat is safe, not just the organizations that impose and enforce rules and regulations for farmers, grocery stores, and food manufacturers.

So, how do you know if something is OK to eat? Do you smell it? Do you check to see if something is growing on it, like mold? Smelling a food might not always work. What about that bottle of barbeque sauce that's been hiding in the back of your refrigerator? It doesn't smell funny, and there is nothing growing on it, so it must be OK to eat, right? Not so fast.

You may be tempted to sniff, poke, and maybe even taste a food to determine if it's safe to eat, but these behaviors could put you at risk. According to the CDC, each year more than seventy-six million Americans get sick with foodborne illnesses, most commonly known

Following simple food safety rules, like checking to see when a food has passed its "Use by" or "Best by" dates, will keep you safe and healthy.

as food poisoning. More than five thousand people die of these illnesses. In almost all cases, they could have been prevented. Many of those illnesses are the result of improper food handling at home, which includes eating food that has spent too much time on the refrigerator shelf or in the back of a pantry. To make sure your food is safe to eat, check food labels and throw out anything that has passed its "Use by" or "Best by" dates. If there are no dates on the food, then be safe and throw it out.

Some Simple Food Safety Rules

How do you prevent yourself and your family from getting sick? Just follow some simple rules:

- Keep hot foods hot. If a food is cooked and put out to serve, make sure that you keep the food hot if it is not going to be eaten right away. If you are going to cool the food in the refrigerator, be sure to cool it quickly in a shallow container.

Perishable food should never be kept at temperatures between 40°F and 140°F (4.4°C and 60°C) for more than two hours. Bacteria can grow quickly at these temperatures and may grow to levels that could cause illness.

- Keep cold foods cold. Cold salads such as macaroni or potato salad, luncheon meats, dairy products, and other foods that require refrigeration should always be kept cold, at temperatures below 40°F (4.4°C). If they are allowed to warm up, bacteria may be able to grow to dangerous levels.
- Wash your hands before handling food. Our hands naturally carry bacteria on them. If we transfer the bacteria from our hands to the food we eat, the bacteria could begin to grow. But the same is true in reverse. If you pick up an apple that hasn't been washed and then you pick up a fork, you could be spreading the bacteria that was on the apple to the fork. So, make sure you wash your hands before and after you handle food. Foods contain a certain amount of bacteria on them as well, especially raw foods such as meat. It is important not to let the bacteria from raw foods stay on your hands, where you may spread the bacteria to your mouth, to other foods, or to objects in your home, like utensils, the kitchen counter, or even a doorknob.

By using separate cutting boards for meat and vegetables, you can eliminate any cross-contamination that might occur, which can lead to the spread of bacteria.

- Don't cross-contaminate. Cross-contamination means infecting one item by touching it to another item that has been infected. This occurs in kitchens when you cook with a lot of different utensils and types of foods. Say you are making beef stew. When you cut up the meat, you might use a cutting board. If the raw meat has some bacteria on it and you use the cutting board to then chop up vegetables, you may have contaminated your vegetables with bacteria that had been on the meat, all because they shared the same cutting board. When you are cooking meat and poultry, you must cook it thoroughly enough to kill any harmful bacteria that may be on it. But even if you cook it correctly, you must make sure you don't let any of the meat's juices get on any other area of your kitchen, such as your countertop, stove, handles to your cupboards, or appliances. These juices, especially when the meat is raw, can contaminate areas of your kitchen, causing illness. If you aren't careful, harmful bacteria can get onto foods that you don't cook before you eat them, like raw vegetables, cheese, and sandwich bread.

General Approaches to Prevention

The FDA stresses prevention as the main way to avoid getting sick. Its Ounce of Prevention campaign targets educators and consumers and arms them with information and useful tips on how best to prevent the spread of infectious diseases. The campaign's goal is to provide information about the importance of hand washing, cleaning, and disinfecting frequently used areas in your home, such as the kitchen. It offers many other easy-to-follow steps in an effort to teach healthy hygiene and cleaning practices. These are the best defenses against the spread of illnesses, like food poisoning.

There are a number of illnesses that can result from unsafe food, but there are three particularly dangerous ones. Botulism is a serious illness caused by a toxin that is produced by the bacteria *Clostridium botulinum*. When this bacteria contaminates food, it can be especially dangerous and can make people very sick. *Campylobacter* bacteria is the second-most frequently reported cause of foodborne illness and is usually caused by consuming unpasteurized milk, raw or undercooked meat or poultry, contaminated foods, and contaminated water. *E. coli* is another leading cause of foodborne illness. Most *E. coli* illness has been associated with eating contaminated ground beef that has been undercooked. People have also become ill by *E. coli* from eating contaminated bean sprouts or fresh leafy vegetables such as lettuce and spinach.

Like the FDA, the FSIS also has a campaign to promote food safety education. It's the Be Food Safe campaign. Created to help people become aware of the dangers of foodborne illness, the Be Food Safe campaign highlights the ways in which food-related illnesses can be prevented. The campaign stresses four key messages: clean, separate, cook, and chill:

- Clean: Wash hands, utensils, and cutting boards before and after contact with raw meat, poultry, seafood, and eggs.
- Separate: Keep raw meat and poultry separate from foods that won't be cooked.
- Cook: Use a food thermometer because you can't always tell food is cooked safely by how it looks.
- Chill: Refrigerate or freeze leftovers and takeout foods within two hours and keep the fridge at 40°F (4.4°C) or below.

The FSIS has also produced a magazine to make available the most up-to-date information on food safety. It's called *be FoodSafe: The FSIS Magazine*. This publication, which comes out four times a year, is full of information on food safety behavior, science and research, inspection issues, and education programs for teachers.

Making sure you cook meat long enough is an easy way to avoid foodborne illness. Use a meat thermometer and check the internal temperature of meat and poultry before serving.

Prevention at Home

Some forms of food poisoning are unavoidable. For example, you have no way of knowing if your food has been cross-contaminated by a restaurant employee with unwashed hands when you eat out. But there are still a number of steps you can take to avoid the most common sources of food poisoning at home.

- Avoid purchasing canned goods that are dented or damaged, as this could be an indication of the presence of botulism toxin.

- Avoid eating in restaurants that appear dirty or that are cited for health code violations.
- Wash your hands in hot, soapy water before and after preparing food.
- Wash cutting boards, knives, utensils, and countertops with hot, soapy water after each use.
- Cook roasts and steaks to at least a temperature of 145°F (63°C) (the core temperature of the meat, not the temperature at which the oven is set). Use a meat thermometer to make sure the core temperature has reached this high.
- Cook ground meat and poultry to at least a temperature of 180°F (82°C).
- Cook eggs until both the yolk and the egg white are firm, not runny.
- Leftovers should be reheated to a temperature of at least 160°F (71°C).
- After microwaving foods, check to make sure there are no cold spots, since bacteria can survive the microwaving process.

Following these simple guidelines should keep you safe from foodborne illnesses and allow you to focus on what really matters—how delicious your meal tastes!

Advances in Food Safety

A mericans are able to enjoy one of the safest food supplies in the world because of such agencies as the USDA, FSIS, and FDA. However, these agencies are always looking for ways to make the food supply even safer. As a result, the FDA has developed the comprehensive Food Protection Plan, which addresses the changes in food sources, production, and consumption that we face in today's world.

The Food Protection Plan

Right now, people are eating a wider range of foods than ever before. We eat more imported foods, and we purchase more exotic cuisine from restaurants and supermarkets. The FDA's plan addresses both the unintentional and deliberate contamination of the nation's food supply by building on current policies and seeking new ways to improve the food safety protections already in place. While there is no solid evidence to

Maine senator Susan Collins makes her opening statement during a Senate hearing with the Food Safety and Inspection Service and the FDA. The hearing discussed the safety of foods being imported into the United States from foreign countries.

suggest that foodborne illness has increased in recent years, this plan only serves to strengthen an already-superior food safety system that has been in place for decades. The Food Protection Plan has three approaches to make sure that what you eat remains safe: prevention, intervention, and response.

The Food Protection Plan stresses prevention. The FDA is seeking to place a greater emphasis on prevention by increasing its interaction with the farmers that grow foods, the manufacturers that make foods, the distributors that deliver foods to supermarkets and stores, the retailers and food service providers that sell foods, and the importers who bring foods to the United States from other countries. By building these partnerships, the FDA will be able to put in place a number of preventive approaches to new safety requirements. By going directly to the growers and producers, the FDA is building safety into the process from the very beginning, reducing your risk of eating food that could make you sick. As part of its prevention approach, it plans to continue to work with state, local, and foreign governments to develop both the tools and the science needed to identify weak spots in the food supply.

The FDA will work with other federal food safety agencies and state, local, and foreign governments to undertake interventions when necessary. These interventions include inspections, testing, and verification that preventative steps are being taken. Intervention also means that the FDA will work with scientists to develop faster food sample testing. So, if a recall needs to take place, it and other government agencies can step in immediately and reduce the risk to as many people as possible.

Responding quickly to a potentially harmful food-borne disease outbreak could mean the difference between life and death for those who have eaten contaminated food. Working with its food safety partners, the FDA is seeking to improve its responses to more rapidly react when indicators arise of either potential or actual harm to a consumer. As part of an improved response system, the FDA will develop faster and more comprehensive ways to communicate with consumers and others during a food-related emergency.

New Technology

The development of new technology, along with the implementation of technology that is already in development, will allow inspectors to identify risk-based factors more quickly. These tools include real-time diagnostic instruments and methods that allow for rapid, on-site analysis of a particular sample. This type of technology could, in some cases, reduce analysis time from days to minutes.

Another way to do a better job is to take the laboratory to the farm, slaughterhouse, or food processing plant. The GoodFood Project aims to do just that by using the latest technology to develop portable devices that can detect contaminates in food products on the spot. Food samples would no longer have to be sent to a laboratory for tests. Instead, foods could be analyzed for safety on farms, during transport or storage, in a processing or packaging plant, or even in a supermarket.

Another advancement in food safety technology is agricultural biotechnology. This field offers a range of tools that alter living organisms such as plants and animals in order to make or modify products and improve the nutritional content of plants or animals. Biotechnology gives farmers tools that can make food production less expensive and more manageable. These biotechnology advances may provide consumers with foods that are nutritionally enriched or

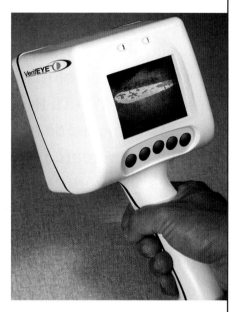

This handheld device, called a VerifEYE, is used to expose food contamination that is invisible to the naked eye.

longer lasting, and they may reduce the levels of certain naturally occurring toxins in some food plants. Developers are using biotechnology to try to reduce saturated fats in cooking oils, reduce allergens, and increase disease-fighting nutrients in foods. The FDA and FSIS oversee agricultural biotechnology to ensure that any bio-altered crops or animals are still safe for you to eat.

Going Organic

Today, with an increase in the number of products grown and produced organically, almost your entire diet can be organic. Currently, more than 73 percent of supermarkets in the United States carry organic foods, with the sales of these foods growing by 17 percent each year. What's the draw?

Organic foods are healthier for you because they have been treated with few, if any, pesticides. Organic foods are produced according to very specific production standards. Organic crops are grown without the use of pesticides and artificial fertilizers and are processed without radiation or food additives. In most countries, organic produce must not be genetically modified either. Meat is certified as organic when animals are raised without the use of antibiotics and growth hormones. In the United States, the USDA's National Organic Program regulates the standards for agricultural products sold as organically produced.

Many supermarkets have an organic section. In it, you might notice three different labels on your foods: "100 Percent Organic," "Organic," and "Made with Organic Ingredients." According to the labeling and marketing information available on the National Organic Program Web site, products labeled "100 Percent Organic" must contain only organically produced ingredients. Products labeled "Organic" must consist of at least 95 percent organically produced ingredients, with the remaining 5 percent of ingredients consisting of agricultural products that are not commercially available in organic form. Products that contain at least 70 percent organic ingredients can use the phrase "Made with Organic Ingredients." These products may include soup, for example, which may have only organic vegetables in it, but the broth and seasonings may not be organic.

Partnership for Food Safety Education

The Partnership for Food Safety Education is a not-for-profit organization that unites the federal government and more than twenty associations and nonprofit organizations, including consumer organizations, food industry associations, commodity groups, and professional associations in the food sciences and nutrition. Their shared goal is to educate the public about safe food handling.

The partnership reaches out to the public in a number of ways, including community outreach, curriculum for teachers to educate students about food safety, radio advertisements to spread the word about food safety, food preparation tips, outreach to supermarkets, and campaigns that stress food safety. Its main campaign, Fight BAC!, was discussed in chapter 1. It also has two other campaigns. Be Food Safe stresses proper food handling and preparation. Safe Produce Handling includes educational materials on safe produce handling, as well as ideas for community outreach.

Myths and Facts

Myth: If you drop a piece of food and pick it up in five seconds or less, it's OK to eat it.

Fact: False. Believe it or not, scientists have tested this rule and found that bacteria can attach itself to your food in only a few seconds. You should never eat food that has fallen to the floor. Even if a floor looks clean, it most likely isn't. Bacteria can live on the floor's surface for a long time, and, once it attaches itself to a food item, it may make you sick. Play it safe and always throw out food that has fallen to the floor.

Myth: If it smells and tastes OK, it must be safe to eat.

Fact: False. It's impossible to use your sense of smell, taste, or sight to tell if a food is safe to eat. Many foods that have started to grow bacteria still look and smell OK. It doesn't take much to make you sick. It only takes as few as ten microscopic bacteria, such as *E. coli*, to cause some food-borne illnesses.

Myth: If you get sick from something you've eaten, it was probably caused by the most recent food item you ate.

Fact: False. It can take half an hour to sometimes as long as six weeks to become sick from unsafe foods. Usually, people feel fine immediately after eating the food and become sick later.

Myth: Meat and poultry should be washed before cooking.

Fact: False. Washing or rinsing meat and poultry before cooking is not necessary, nor is it recommended. In fact, washing increases the danger of cross-contamination, spreading bacteria present on the surface of meat and poultry to other foods, kitchen utensils, counter surfaces, and most important, the sink you used to wash the food in. Cooking meat and poultry to the recommended temperatures will make them safe to eat.

Myth: As long as the lid is on a food item that has sat out too long, it is still safe to eat.

Fact: False. Although food may be safe after cooking, it may not be safe after cooling down. Just one bacterium in the food can double in twenty minutes, and as many as two million bacteria can grow on a food item left at room temperature for seven hours. Refrigerate perishable foods within two hours at 40°F (4.4°C) or lower.

Glossary

agricultural inspectors Government employees who inspect food production facilities and farms, and test and sample food products to ensure they are safe.

antibiotics Medicines that inhibit or kill microorganisms that can cause illness in people and animals.

cross-contaminate To infect something by contact or association with another item.

export To send an item, like food, to another country.

foodborne illness Any illness resulting from the consumption of food. Foodborne illnesses are most commonly referred to as food poisoning.

growth hormone A substance that stimulates rapid growth in humans and animals.

hygiene Conditions or practices that encourage cleanliness and good health.

import To bring an item, like food, into a country.

organic Grown without the use of pesticides and artificial fertilizers, and processed without using radiation or food additives. Organic meat is produced from animals raised without the use of antibiotics and growth hormones.

pasteurization Heating a food at a temperature and for a period of time sufficient to destroy harmful bacteria without effecting major changes to the original substance.

perishable An item that is likely to spoil or decay.

recall To order the return of items to stores or manufacturers because they have something wrong with them and may pose a danger to consumers.

sanitation The science and practice of creating healthy and hygienic conditions.

shelf life The period of time during which a material may be stored and remain suitable for use.

tween A blend of the words "between" and "teenager"; refers to a child between the ages of eight and thirteen.

For More Information

Canadian Food Inspection Agency
59 Camelot Drive
Ottawa, ON K1A 0Y9
Canada
(800) 442-2342
Web site: http://www.inspection.gc.ca/english/toce.shtml
The Canadian Food Inspection Agency is dedicated to
    safeguarding food, animals, and plants, which
    enhances the health and well-being of Canada's
    people, environment, and economy.

Canadian Institute of Food Science and Technology
3-1750 The Queensway, Suite 1311
Toronto, ON M9C 5H5
Canada
(905) 271-8338
Web site: http://www.cifst.ca
The Canadian Institute of Food Science and Technology
    is Canada's national association for food industry
    professionals. Its membership of more than 1,200
    includes scientists and technologists in industry,
    government, and academia who are committed to
    advancing food science and technology.

Center for Food Safety
660 Pennsylvania Avenue SE, Suite 302
Washington, DC 20003
(202) 547-9359
Web site: http://www.centerforfoodsafety.org
The Center for Food Safety is a nonprofit public interest
    and environmental advocacy membership organiza-
    tion established by the International Center for
    Technology Assessment. The center's purpose is to
    challenge harmful food production technologies and
    promote sustainable alternatives.

Food Safety Information Center
National Agricultural Library
10301 Baltimore Avenue, Room 304
Beltsville, MD 20705
(301) 504-6835
Web site: http://foodsafety.nal.usda.gov
The Food Safety Information Center specializes in
    providing food safety information to educators,
    industry, researchers, and the general public.

International Food Information Council Foundation
1100 Connecticut Avenue NW, Suite 430
Washington, DC 20036
(202) 296-6540

Web site: http://www.ific.org

The International Food Information Council Foundation's mission is to communicate science-based information on food safety and nutrition to health and nutrition professionals, educators, journalists, government officials, and others providing information to consumers.

Web Sites

Due to the changing nature of Internet links, Rosen Publishing has developed an online list of Web sites related to the subject of this book. This site is updated regularly. Please use this link to access this list:

http://www.rosenlinks.com/itn/sfs

For Further Reading

Entis, Phyllis. *Food Safety: Old Habits and New Perspectives.* Washington, DC: ASM Press, 2007.

Kallen, Stuart A. *Food Safety* (At Issue). Farmington Hills, MI: Greenhaven Press, 2004.

McSwane, David, Richard Linton, and Nancy R. Rue. *Essentials of Food Safety and Sanitation.* Upper Saddle River, NJ: Prentice Hall, 2004.

Nestle, Marion. *Safe Food: Bacteria, Biotechnology, and Bioterrorism.* Berkeley, CA: University of California Press, 2004.

Nestle, Marion. *What to Eat.* New York, NY: North Point Press, 2007.

Roberts, Cynthia A. *The Food Safety Information Handbook.* Phoenix, AZ: Oryx Press, 2001.

Schmidt, Ronald H., and Gary G. Rodrick. *Food Safety Handbook.* Hoboken, NJ: Wiley, 2002.

Bibliography

Azonano.com. "Tiny Devices to Feed Advances in Food Safety." Retrieved March 2, 2008 (http://www.azonano.com/news.asp?newsID=1884).

Beier, Ross C., et al., eds. *Preharvest and Postharvest Food Safety: Contemporary Issues and Future Directions*. Hoboken, NJ: Wiley-Blackwell, 2004.

CNN.com. "*E. Coli* Spinach Scare Increases to 21 States." September 19, 2006. Retrieved February 18, 2008 (http://www.cnn.com/2006/HEALTH/09/18/tainted.spinach/index.html).

CNN.com. "FDA OKs Meat, Milk from Most Cloned Animals." January 15, 2008. Retrieved March 2, 2008 (http://www.cnn.com/2008/HEALTH/01/15/fda.cloning/index.html).

CNN.com. "Pet Food Scare: Details on Recall." April 17, 2007. Retrieved March 2, 2008 (http://www.cnn.com/2007/US/04/02/recall.links/index.html).

FDA.gov. "FDA Warning on Serious Food-Borne *E. Coli* O157:H7 Outbreak." September 14, 2006. Retrieved February 18, 2008 (http://www.fda.gov/bbs/topics/NEWS/2006/NEW01450.html).

FDA.gov. "Milestones in U.S. Food and Drug Law History." May 3, 1999. Retrieved March 2, 2008 (http://www.fda.gov/opacom/backgrounders/miles.html).

FDA.gov. "Spot the Block: Using the Nutrition Facts Label to Make Healthy Food Choices—A Program for Tweens." Retrieved March 9, 2007 (http://www.cfsan.fda.gov/~dms/spotcaag.html).

FDA.gov. "The Story of the Laws Behind the Labels." Retrieved February 1, 2008 (http://www.cfsan.fda.gov/~lrd/history1.html).

FoodProtection.org. "About the International Association for Food Protection." Retrieved March 2, 2008 (http://www.foodprotection.org/aboutIAFP/whoweare.asp).

FoodSafety.gov. "Celebrating National Food Safety Month." Retrieved February 18, 2008 (http://www.foodsafety.gov/~fsg/fs-mon07.html).

Goldberg, Adam. "Consumers Union Research Team Shows: Organic Foods Really DO Have Less Pesticides." ConsumersUnion.org, May 8, 2002. Retrieved March 2, 2008 (http://www.consumersunion.org/food/organicpr.htm).

International Food Information Council. "Agricultural Practices & Food Technologies." November 2006. Retrieved February 18, 2008 (http://www.ific.org/food/agriculture/index.cfm).

Nestle, Marion. *Food Politics: How the Food Industry Influences Nutrition and Health*. Berkeley, CA: University of California Press, 2007.

Raine, George. "San Benito County Ranch Source of Tainted Spinach." *San Francisco Chronicle*, March 23,

2007. Retrieved February 18, 2008 (http://www.
sfgate.com/cgi-bin/article.cgi?f=/c/a/2007/03/23/
BAGJDOQM1H8.DTL).

Roberts, Cynthia A. *Food Safety Information Handbook.*
Westport, CT: Oryx Press, 2001.

Spencer, Naomi. "Largest Beef Recall in U.S. History
Reveals Compromised Food Supply." WSWS.org,
February 19, 2008. Retrieved March 2, 2008 (http://
www.wsws.org/articles/2008/feb2008/beef-f19.shtml).

Torrence, Mary E., and Richard E. Isaac. *Microbial Food
Safety in Animal Agriculture: Current Topics.*
Hoboken, NJ: Wiley-Blackwell, 2003.

USDA.gov. "Food Safety Facts." Retrieved February 29,
2008 (http://www.fsis.usda.gov/Fact_Sheets/
Irradiation_and_Food_Safety/index.asp).

USDA.gov. "Labeling and Marketing Information."
Retrieved March 2, 2008 (http://www.ams.usda.gov/
nop/FactSheets/LabelingE.html).

Weiss, Rick. "FDA Is Set to Approve Milk, Meat from
Clones?" WashingtonPost.com, October 17, 2006.
Retrieved February 18, 2008 (http://www.
washingtonpost.com/wp-dyn/content/arti-
cle/2006/10/16/AR2006101601337_pf.html).

Whitman, Deborah B. "Genetically Modified Foods:
Harmful or Helpful?" CSA.com, April 2000.
Retrieved February 18, 2008 (http://www.csa.com/
discoveryguides/gmfood/overview.php).

Index

About the Author

Laura La Bella is a writer who lives and works in Rochester, New York. Since completing this book, she has joined efforts to persuade New York State's congressional and senatorial leadership to support the labeling of all foods that contain genetically engineered ingredients.

Photo Credits

Cover (top left), p. 38 Shutterstock.com; cover (top right), pp. 30, 31, 37, 40, 43 USDA; cover (bottom) www.istockphoto.com/alohaspirit; pp. 4, 10 Library of Congress Prints and Photographs Division; p. 5 Justin Sullivan/ Getty Images; p. 7 Mark Wilson/Getty Images; p. 11 Bill Pugliano/Getty Images; p. 12 © The Partnership for Food Safety Education; pp. 15, 18, 25 © AP Images; p. 16 Fox Photos/Getty Images; pp. 24, 29 Joe Raedle/ Getty Images; p. 28 Chip Somodevilla/Getty Images; p. 33 © rollcallpix/ Newscom; p. 34 © KRT News/Newscom; pp. 45, 46 Douglas Graham/ Congressional Quarterly/Getty Images; p. 49 PRNewsFoto/Newscom.

Designer: Tom Forget; Photo Researcher: Amy Feinberg